10|9

D0382570

MANCOS
PUBLIC LIBRARY
Severance Middle School
Media Center

A PRIMARY SOURCE HISTORY
OF THE UNITED STATES

THE ERA OF RECONSTRUCTION AND EXPANSION

1865–1900

George E. Stanley

WORLD ALMANAC® LIBRARY

Please visit our web site at: www.worldalmanaclibrary.com
For a free color catalog describing World Almanac® Library's list of high-quality
books and multimedia programs, call 1-800-848-2928 (USA) or 1-800-387-3178
(Canada). World Almanac® Library's fax: (414) 332-3567.

Library of Congress Cataloging-in-Publication Data available upon request from publisher.
Fax (414) 336-0157 for the attention of the Publishing Records Department.

ISBN 0-8368-5827-1 (lib. bdg.)
ISBN 0-8368-5836-0 (softcover)

First published in 2005 by
World Almanac® Library
330 West Olive Street, Suite 100
Milwaukee, WI 53212 USA

Copyright © 2005 by World Almanac® Library.

Produced by Byron Preiss Visual Publications Inc.
Project Editor: Susan Hoe
Designer: Marisa Gentile
World Almanac® Library editor: Alan Wachtel
World Almanac® Library art direction: Tammy West

Picture acknowledgements:
Library of Congress: Cover (lower left), pp. 5, 7, 8, 10, 11, 12, 13, 15, 17, 19, 21, 23,
25 (top right), 25 (bottom left), 27, 28, 30, 32, 33, 35, 36, 37, 40, 41, 42 and 43;
The Granger Collection, New York: Cover (upper left, upper right, lower right), p. 20;
Picture History: p. 9.

All rights reserved. No part of this book may be reproduced, stored in a retrieval system,
or transmitted in any form or by any means, electronic, mechanical, photocopying,
recording, or otherwise, without the prior written permission of the copyright holder.

Printed in the United States of America

1 2 3 4 5 6 7 8 9 09 08 07 06 05

Dr. George E. Stanley is a professor at Cameron University in Lawton, Oklahoma. He has authored
more than eighty books for young readers, many in the field of history and science. Dr. Stanley recently
completed a series of history books on famous Americans, including *Geronimo, Andrew Jackson,
Harry S. Truman*, and *Mr. Rogers*.

CONTENTS

Through the examination of authentic historical documents, including charters, diaries, journals, letters, speeches, and other written records, each title in *A Primary Source History of the United States* offers a unique perspective on the events that shaped the United States. In addition to providing important historical information, each document serves as a piece of living history that opens a window into the kinds of thinking and modes of expression that characterized the various epochs of American history.

Note: To facilitate the reading of older documents, the modern-day spelling of certain words is used.

CHAPTER 1

Reconstruction

1865–1877

The period of Reconstruction at the end of the Civil War covered the years between the surrender of the Confederate forces in 1865 and the removal of the last Union occupation troops in 1877. During this time, the South was the scene of bitter strife, as its status within the Union and the plans for its rebuilding were debated. But in the end, new patterns of government, economy, and society emerged that would transform the Southern states.

More than a year before the Civil War ended, President Lincoln devised a plan to restore the Confederate states to the Union. He called the plan his Proclamation of Amnesty and Reconstruction. It required ten percent of a state's voters to accept emancipation of the slaves and to take an oath of allegiance to the United States, before that state could return to the Union.

Some members of Congress thought Lincoln's plan was too generous. They preferred the Wade-Davis Bill, which called for a military government in each state and required at least fifty percent of eligible voters to swear allegiance to the United States. Neither plan was accepted. Just before Lincoln's death, however, Congress passed the Thirteenth

THIRTEENTH AMENDMENT: 1865

Section 1. Neither slavery nor involuntary servitude, except as a punishment for crime whereof the party shall have been duly convicted, shall exist within the United States, or any place subject to their jurisdiction.
Section 2. Congress shall have power to enforce this article by appropriate legislation.

Amendment to the Constitution, which pronounced slavery unconstitutional and expanded on the Emancipation Proclamation.

In retaliation against the Thirteenth Amendment, many of the Southern slave states adopted so-called black codes. These laws were specifically intended to keep the newly freed slaves in a subservient role.

ANDREW JOHNSON ASSUMES OFFICE

Following Lincoln's assassination, the job of overseeing Reconstruction fell to President Andrew Johnson. In May 1865, with Congress out of session, Johnson began to implement his own plan whereby the Southern states would be admitted back into the Union. He granted amnesty to all

MISSISSIPPI BLACK CODES: 1865

... If any person shall persuade or attempt to persuade ... any freedman, free negro, or mulatto to desert from the legal employment of any person before the expiration of his or her term of service ... he shall be guilty of a misdemeanor....

That no freedman, free negro or mulatto, not in the military service ... shall keep or carry fire-arms of any kind....

◀An 1865 wood engraving shows Andrew Johnson being sworn into office after the death of President Lincoln.

former Confederates—except certain high-ranking leaders and large property holders—who were willing to take an oath to uphold the Constitution. He issued proclamations that set up provisional governments in the former Confederate states. He authorized all loyal white citizens to draft and ratify new state constitutions and to elect state legislatures, but he outlined exactly what they were required to do to rejoin the Union: repeal the ordinances of secession, repudiate the Confederate state debts, and ratify the Thirteenth Amendment to the Constitution.

Those members of the Republican party who opposed President Johnson's reconstruction plan were known as Radicals, and they dominated the Congress that convened in December 1865. The group was led by Senator Charles Sumner of Massachusetts and Representative Thaddeus Stevens of Pennsylvania.

The Radical Republicans were stymied by their inability to control Johnson, and they began to fear that the executive branch of the government was starting to encroach on the authority of Congress. The Radical Republicans wanted to safeguard the interests of blacks freed from slavery as a result of the Civil War, and they

resented the return so soon of former Confederate politicians to power in the South. By removing the southern influence in Congress, many Radical Republicans hoped to establish their own party in the South.

A new Civil Rights Act was passed in 1866, but there were doubts that it could be enforced, so Congress drafted the Fourteenth Amendment to the Constitution. In effect, this amendment nullified the Supreme Court's 1857 *Dred Scott* v. *Sandford* decision and declared that all blacks were citizens of the United States and as such would be given equal protection under the law.

Congress felt the policies of President Johnson were too lenient on the Southern states, so it enacted the Reconstruction Act on March 2, 1867, which divided the South into

FOURTEENTH AMENDMENT: 1868

Section 1. All persons born or naturalized in the United States, and subject to the jurisdiction thereof, are citizens of the United States and of the state wherein they reside....

THE FIRST RECONSTRUCTION ACT: 1867

Whereas no legal State governments … now exist in the rebel States of Virginia, North Carolina, South Carolina, Georgia, Mississippi, Alabama, Louisiana, Florida, Texas, and Arkansas [Tennessee was excluded because it had ratified the Fourteenth Amendment]; and whereas it is necessary that peace and good order should be enforced in said States until loyal and republican State governments can be legally established: Therefore … said rebel States shall be divided into military districts and made subject to the military authority of the United States.…

"… rebel States shall be divided into military districts.… "

military districts, with Union soldiers to protect the rights of blacks.

Some of the state legislatures worked hard to be readmitted to the Union, but their readmission hinged on their ratifying the Fifteenth Amendment, which guaranteed blacks the right to vote.

Susan B. Anthony and Elizabeth Cady Stanton, women's rights advocates, were angry that the amendment did not also list gender as a condition to deny a citizen the right to vote. Actually, Congress had carefully worded this amendment so that Northern states could also continue to deny voting rights to women and certain groups of men, such as Chinese immigrants, illiterates, and those too poor to pay poll taxes.

▲ A photograph of Susan B. Anthony taken between 1890 and 1910.

FIFTEENTH AMENDMENT: 1869

Section 1. The right of citizens of the United States to vote shall not be denied or abridged by the United States or by any State on account of race, color, or previous condition of servitude.

Section 2. The Congress shall have power to enforce this article by appropriate legislation.

IMPEACHMENT

Because of Congress's displeasure with President Johnson, it tried to limit presidential power by passing the Tenure of Office Act in 1867, which forbade Johnson to fire any federal employee. In February 1868, the House of Representatives voted to impeach the president on the grounds that he had violated the act, but Johnson was acquitted.

▲ An 1868 wood engraving depicting the impeachment trial of Andrew Johnson. The court was held on the floor of the Senate.

Ku Klux Klan

By 1868, most Southern states had ratified the Fourteenth Amendment. Many unhappy Southern whites formed secret societies that tried to undo the results of Reconstruction and to restore "white supremacy." The Ku Klux Klan was the most notorious of these organizations. Members wore white hoods and robes and went on night raids, where they terrorized blacks and their white supporters. In 1870 and 1871, Congress passed the Enforcement Acts, which were intended to enforce the Fourteenth Amendment and to put an end to the Ku Klux Klan and other secret societies.

▲ An 1868 illustration of two members of the Ku Klux Klan holding a rifle and pistol.

Enforcement Acts: 1870 and 1871

Civil Rights Act of 1870
... It shall be the duty of every person and officer to give to all citizens of the United States the ... opportunity ... to become qualified to vote without distinction of race, color, or previous condition of servitude....

Civil Rights Act of 1871
... If two or more persons within any State or Territory of the United States shall ... go in disguise upon the public highway or upon the premises of another for the purpose, either directly or indirectly, of depriving any person or any class of person of the equal protection of the laws ... each and every person so offending shall be deemed guilty of a high crime....

SEWARD'S FOLLY

As people put the Civil War behind them, there was renewed pressure for expansion. In 1867, however, when Secretary of State William H. Seward arranged for the United States to buy the vast territory known as Alaska from the Russian government for $7.2 million, he was ridiculed. Many people thought it was a waste of money and referred to Alaska as "Seward's Folly." But Seward was able to convince important congressmen of Alaska's economic potential, and others were swayed by what they viewed as the dawning of a friendship with Russia.

A treaty ceding all Russian possessions in North America to the United States was signed by His Majesty, Alexander II, the Emperor of all the Russias, on June 20, 1867.

TREATY TO PURCHASE ALASKA: 1867

… His Majesty the Emperor of all the Russias agrees to cede to the United States … all the territory and dominion now possessed by his said Majesty on the continent of America and in the adjacent islands.…

In consideration of the cession aforesaid, the United States agree to pay … seven million two hundred thousand dollars in gold.…

ULYSSES S. GRANT

Ulysses S. Grant, the general who had accepted Lee's surrender at the end of the Civil War, was elected president in 1868, but his naiveté and lack of political experience proved to be a handicap to both him and the nation. Neither by training nor by temperament was he qualified to set a high standard of political ethics. His brother-in-law was involved in a plot to corner the gold market, and his vice president, Schuyler Colfax, was involved in a scheme that skimmed profits from the Union Pacific Railroad Company.

▲ A photocopy of the check, in the amount of $7.2 million, that was issued to Russia for the purchase of Alaska in 1868.

ULYSSES S. GRANT'S FIRST INAUGURAL ADDRESS: 1869

... The country having just emerged from a great rebellion, many questions will come before it for settlement in the next four years which preceding Administrations have never had to deal with. In meeting these it is desirable that they should be approached calmly, without prejudice, hate, or sectional pride, remembering that the greatest good to the greatest number is the object to be attained....

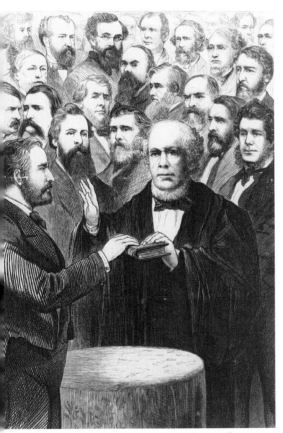

▲ This 1873 wood engraving shows Grant taking the oath of office at his inauguration.

Despite all of President Grant's problems, he was reelected in 1872. That year, Congress passed the General Amnesty Act, removing almost all restrictions against former Confederate officials. The country viewed this act as the end of Reconstruction.

Unfortunately for the nation, Grant's admiration for and association with some wealthy but dishonest men allowed government graft to continue. Secretary of War William Belknap resigned in disgrace for taking bribes from dishonest Indian agents, and Grant's personal secretary helped a group of distillers avoid paying taxes. By 1876, the Republicans sought a presidential candidate that was untouched by the scandals of the Grant administration. They chose Ohio governor Rutherford B. Hayes.

CHAPTER 2

Development of the West

1865–1900

After the Civil War, millions of white settlers crossed the western plains and the mountains by wagon train in hopes of finding a better life. From the beginning, these settlers and the Indians of the West misunderstood each other's cultures. Most of the tribes claimed the plains as their ancestral hunting grounds. The settlers viewed the Indians as savages and barriers to civilization.

THE INDIAN WARS

As new territories and states were organized, the United States government decided to establish reservations for each tribe and to encourage the Indians to take up farming. While some Indian groups did settle on the small tracts of land allotted to them, others resisted. Between 1862 and 1890, there were a series of battles between the various tribes and the United States Army. These battles were known collectively as the Indian Wars.

▲ This 1877 wood engraving depicts various scenes of the United States Army and the Nez Percé Indians.

In 1877, the U.S. government ordered the Nez Percé tribe to move to a reservation in Idaho. Chief Joseph agreed, but after some of his men killed a group of white settlers, he tried to escape to Canada with his people. The United States Army pursued and captured them. On October 5, 1877, Chief Joseph surrendered in the Bear Paw Mountains.

CHIEF JOSEPH'S SURRENDER: 1877

Tell General Howard that I know his heart. What he told me before I have in my heart. I am tired of fighting. Our chiefs are killed. Looking Glass is dead, Tuhulhilsote is dead. The old men are all dead. It is the young men who now say yes or no. He who led the young men [Chief Joseph's brother Alikut] is dead. It is cold and we have no blankets. The little children are freezing to death. My people—some of them have run away to the hills and have no blankets and no food. No one knows where they are— perhaps freezing to death. I want to have time to look for my children and see how many of them I can find. Maybe I shall find them among the dead. Hear me, my chiefs, my heart is sick and sad. From where the sun now stands I will fight no more forever.

▲ A 1900 photograph of Chief Joseph, wearing his traditional Nez Percé headdress.

★

In 1879, during a trip to Boston, Helen Hunt Jackson heard Ponca chief Standing Bear speak about the plight of the Plains Indians. Later, she wrote a book entitled *A Century of Dishonor*, which condemned the government's treatment of the Indians. She used strong language, such as "... cheating, robbing, breaking promises ..." to describe the action of the government. Some thought her book was capable of doing great harm.

In 1887, the government abandoned its policy of dealing with the tribes as sovereign nations and passed the Dawes Severalty Act, which declared Indians citizens of the United States and granted specified acreage from reservation lands to Indian families for farming. Reservation lands not allotted to Indians were sold to the general public.

THE DAWES SEVERALTY ACT: 1887

66And every Indian born within the territorial limits of the United States ... is hereby declared to be a citizen of the United States....99

... In all cases where any tribe or band of Indians has been ... located upon any reservation ... the President of the United States ... is, authorized, whenever in his opinion any reservation of any part thereof of such Indians is advantageous for agricultural and grazing purposes, to cause said reservation ... to be surveyed ... and to allot the lands in said reservation in severalty to any Indian located thereon in quantities....

And every Indian born within the territorial limits of the United States ... who has voluntarily taken up ... his residence separate and apart from any tribe of Indians therein, and has adopted the habits of civilized life, is hereby declared to be a citizen of the United States....

In the late 1800s, the Indians of the plains, faced with losing their freedom, their homes, and their beliefs, turned to the "Ghost Dance" movement, in a desperate attempt to restore their past and to separate them from the white man. They believed that if all Indians performed the slow shuffling movements to go with the singing and chanting, the white man would disappear and the Indian dead would return, bringing with them the old way of life.

In 1890, Kuwapi, a member of the Rosebud Sioux, was arrested for leading a Ghost Dance. He was interviewed by a federal policeman named Selwyn.

INTERVIEW OF KUWAPI: 1890

The Ghost Dance Religion and the Sioux Outbreak, Bureau of Ethnology, Washington, D.C.

Selwyn: Do you believe in the new messiah?

Kuwapi: I somewhat believe it.

Selwyn: What made you believe it?

Kuwapi: Because I ate some of the buffalo meat that he [the new messiah] sent to the Rosebud Indians through Short Bull....

Selwyn: Do not the Rosebud people prepare to attack the white people this summer?...

Kuwapi: Yes.

Selwyn: You do not mean to say that the Rosebud Indians will try and cause an [insurrection]?

Kuwapi: That seems to be the case....

In December of 1890, the Seventh Cavalry killed more than three hundred Sioux men, women, and children at Wounded Knee Creek, in a battle that lasted less than an hour. This massacre marked the end of Indian resistance in which the Ghost Dance played a major role.

▼ An 1891 print shows the Seventh Calvary battling the Indians at Wounded Knee Creek.

FARMERS MOVE WEST

Government policy and the trains that now crossed the entire continent encouraged the agricultural development of the West. The Homestead Act of 1862 gave 160 acres of land to a family who would farm it for five years.

Under the Timber Culture Act, settlers could get an additional 160 acres if they planted and maintained trees. The Desert Land Act allowed settlers to buy additional acreage at $1.25 per acre if the land was irrigated within three years.

Hamlin Garland, one of the settlers, wrote about his life on the Iowa prairie in a 1917 published book entitled *A Son of the Middle Border.*

A SON OF THE MIDDLE BORDER: 1917

… It burned deep into our memories, this wide, sunny, windy country. The sky so big, and the horizon line so low and so far away, made this new world of the plain … majestic…. On the uplands the herbage was short and dry and the plants stiff and woody, but in the wales the wild oak shook its quivers of barbed and twisted arrows, and the crow's foot, tall and sere, bowed softly under the feet of the wind, while everywhere, in the lowlands as well as on the ridges, the bleaching white antlers of by-gone herbivora lay scattered, testifying to the herds of deer and buffalo which once fed there. We were just a few years too late to see them….

With more new land under cultivation and with the widespread use of machinery, there was a tremendous increase in farm production in the late 1800s. Agriculture, however, failed to bring the wealth that many farmers hoped it would. Unfortunately, those farmers did not understand how the market operated. When prices fell, they planted more of the same crop, which only added to the worldwide surplus and pushed prices still lower. The farmers had borrowed heavily to buy their land and equipment, so with no money coming in, the number of foreclosures increased

"FARMER GREEN'S REAPER": 1874

… The agent was a smooth tongued, plausible fellow, and he plied the farmer with every argument he was master of. The result was that the farmer bought the reaper. He had not the money to pay for it, but he gave what is called in Iowa "an iron-clad note" for it.… By the laws of Iowa such a note is equivalent to a mortgage … so, in order to purchase the reaper, the farmer had imperilled his property.…

Improved machinery is useful where it is honestly made, but … [the farmer's] hard earnings … go to make up colossal fortunes of manufacturers and dealers in such machinery. A reform is needed, and it is near at hand.…

> **"… so, in order to purchase the reaper, the farmer had imperilled his property.…"**

steadily. Farmers usually blamed their plight on others: the railroads for charging too much for freight, the government for keeping the supply of money tight, and middlemen, such as grain-elevator operators, for not paying them enough for their crops.

When Congress refused to help the farmers, they began to organize. The Patrons of Husbandry, or the Grange, was established in 1867. It encouraged farmer-owned cooperatives and helped with their grievances.

Edward Winslow Martin's *History of the Grange Movement* retells the episode of "Farmer Green's Reaper" in which a farmer is smooth-talked into buying a reaper he cannot afford, thereby putting his farm in jeopardy.

▲ This promotional print, c.1873, encouraged Grange members by showing idyllic scenes of farm life.

GOLD ATTRACTS FOREIGN IMMIGRANTS

The discovery of gold in California in 1849 triggered a migration of tens of thousands of people who hoped to make their fortune in the mineral-rich West. Racial discrimination was rife among the diverse populations that sought gold.

Chinese immigrants had flocked to America to escape hunger and poverty in their own land. Many also worked on the building of the Transcontinental Railroad. But as their numbers increased, they became scapegoats for workers who felt the Chinese were taking their jobs and lowering the wage rates. In 1882, Congress passed the Chinese Exclusion Act, which suspended the immigration of Chinese to the United States for a period of ten years.

CHINESE EXCLUSION ACT: 1882

Whereas, in the opinion of the Government of the United States the coming of Chinese laborers to this country endangers the good order of certain localities within the territory thereof: Therefore,

Be it enacted by the Senate and House of Representatives of the United States of America in Congress assembled, That from and after the expiration of ninety days next after the passage of this act, and until the expiration of ten years next after the passage of this act, the coming of Chinese laborers to the United States be, and the same is hereby, suspended....

THE OKLAHOMA LAND RUN

Even though the United States had promised the Cherokee people that they could live in Oklahoma forever, the government decided to open up the land to white settlers in 1889. On April 22, thousands of white settlers waited for the Oklahoma Land Run to begin. When the starting pistol was fired, the settlers rushed to claim their free 160 acres of land.

In 1893, Frederick Jackson Turner, a young historian, presented a paper entitled "The Significance of the Frontier in American History." In it, Turner theorized that the constant rebirth and new struggles endured by each new wave of settlers moving across the western frontier helped to define what was to become the American character.

◀ An 1889 wood engraving showing settlers on horses and wagons racing to claim a piece of land in Oklahoma.

TURNER'S PAPER ON THE AMERICAN FRONTIER: 1893

… Said [John C.] Calhoun in 1817, "We are great, and rapidly—I was about to say fearfully—growing!" So saying, he touched the distinguishing feature of American life…. American development has exhibited not merely advance along a single line, but a return to primitive conditions on a continually advancing frontier line, and a new development for that area. American social development has been continually beginning over again on the frontier. This perennial rebirth, this fluidity of American life, this expansion westward with its new opportunities, its continuous touch with the simplicity of primitive society, furnish the forces dominating American character. The true point of view in the history of this nation is not the Atlantic, it is the great West….

CHAPTER 3

The Rise in Manufacturing

1867–1900

Between 1865, the end of the Civil War, and 1900, the United States underwent a remarkable economic transformation and surpassed all nations. Many manufacturers still made consumer goods, such as footwear, textiles, and furniture. Other manufacturers produced capital goods, such as iron and steel, which were purchased by businesses. This economic growth brought about the beginning of organized labor and the first serious attempts by the federal government to regulate big business.

THE RAILROADS

The Transcontinental Railroad was completed in 1869, when the Union Pacific joined with the Central Pacific Railroad. Although this mighty railroad played a key role in the economic growth of the country, the high rates charged by the different lines led to regulation of the industry.

▼ An 1869 wood engraving shows the historical meeting of the Union Pacific and Central Pacific Railroads.

The Supreme Court ruling of *Wabash* v. *Illinois* established that the transport of goods within a single state would be regulated by that state, but the transport of goods between states (that is, interstate) would be subject to regulations set by Congress. In 1887, Congress passed the Interstate Commerce Act, which stated that interstate railroads could not charge exorbitant rates.

THE STEEL MILLS

Steel also played a major role in the nation's economic development. New technology allowed the amount of steel produced in the United States to increase from seventy-seven thousand tons in 1870 to over ten million tons in 1900. Most of the production came from one company, Carnegie Steel, founded by Andrew Carnegie.

Carnegie was also a philanthropist, who used his immense fortune to support universities, libraries, and hospitals throughout the United States. He wanted to give a larger meaning to his personal success. In an article titled "Wealth," which was published in the *North American Review*, Carnegie expressed his views on the responsibility of the wealthy.

"WEALTH" BY ANDREW CARNEGIE: 1889

... This, then, is held to be the duty of the man of Wealth: First, to set an example of modest, unostentatious living, shunning display or extravagance; to provide moderately for the legitimate wants of those dependent upon him; and after doing so to consider all surplus revenues which come to him simply as trust funds, which he is called upon to administer, and strictly bound as a matter of duty to administer in the manner which, in his judgment, is best calculated to produce the most beneficial results for the community—the man of wealth thus becoming the mere agent and trustee for his poorer brethren, bringing to their service his superior wisdom, experience, and ability to administer, doing for them better than they would or could do for themselves....

▲ A photograph, c.1913, of philanthropist Andrew Carnegie.

RISE OF THE LABOR UNIONS

The greatest natural resource discovery of the nineteenth century was oil. Edwin L. Drake sank his first oil well in Pennsylvania in 1859. By 1890, the United States was producing over fifty million barrels of oil each year.

More than ninety percent of the oil was pumped, refined, and sold by one company—John D. Rockefeller's Standard Oil of Ohio. But Rockefeller's attempt to monopolize the market forced Congress to pass antitrust laws.

SHERMAN ANTITRUST ACT: 1890

... Every contract, combination in the form of trust or otherwise or conspiracy, in restraint of trade or commerce [among the several States, or with foreign nations], is hereby declared to be illegal....

Every person who shall monopolize, or attempt to monopolize, or combine or conspire with any other person or person, to monopolize any part of the trade or commerce among the several States, or with foreign nations, shall be deemed guilty of a misdemeanor, and, on conviction thereof, shall be punished by fine not exceeding five thousand dollars, or by imprisonment not exceeding one year, or by both said punishments, in the discretion of the court....

— ★ —

Fewer than one million people worked in industry before the Civil War, but by the end of the century, that number had tripled, and it included men, women, and children.

Factory workers formed mutual benefit societies to help each other through illness, injury, and death, but they could do little about the most serious problem: unemployment. The labor unions grew out of a need to deal with this problem. In 1886, Samuel Gompers founded the American Federation of Labor. It promoted labor legislation and supported strikes. Between 1880 and 1890, there were over twenty thousand strikes involving almost seven million workers. The Pullman (maker of railroad sleeping cars) Strike of 1894 created a national crisis. The testimony of the vice president of the Pullman Company before the U.S. Strike Commission illustrates the problem union members had being accepted and recognized by management.

TESTIMONY BEFORE THE U.S. STRIKE COMMISSION: 1894

[Commissioner John D.] Kernan: Has the company had any policy with reference to labor unions among its help?

[Thomas H.] Wickes [second vice president of the Pullman Company]: No; we have never objected to unions except in one instance. I presume that there are quite a number of unions in our shops now.

Kernan: What are they?

Wickes: I couldn't tell you, but I have heard of some of them....

Kernan: The only objection you ever made was to the American Railway Union, wasn't it?

Wickes: Yes, sir....

Kernan: Then you think that you have the right to refuse to recognize a union of the men....

Wickes: That is the policy of the company; yes, sir. If we were to receive these men ... they could probably force us to pay any wages which they saw fit....

This 1894 print shows the encampment of U.S. troops during the railroad strikes. ▶

CHAPTER 4

Changes in Urban Life

1867–1900

American society was significantly changed by industrial expansion. As farmers left the rural areas of the country for the city, the nation became increasingly urbanized. The nation's urban growth was also fueled by a mass immigration from Europe and parts of Asia as well as from the Middle East.

This ever-growing industrialization and urbanization left its mark on the daily lives of the people living in cities. In *How the Other Half Lives*, Jacob A. Riis describes how cosmopolitan New York City already was by the late nineteenth century and illustrates some of the negative racial attitudes that people held at the time.

HOW THE OTHER HALF LIVES: 1890

… When once I asked the agent of a notorious Fourth Ward alley how many people might be living in it I was told: One hundred and forty families, one hundred Irish, thirty-eight Italian, and two that spoke the German tongue. Barring the agent herself, there was not a native-born individual in the court. The answer was characteristic of the cosmopolitan character of lower New York, very nearly so of the whole of it…. One may find for the asking an Italian, a German, a French, African, Spanish, Bohemian, Russian, Scandinavian, Jewish, and Chinese colony. Even the Arab, who peddles "holy earth" from the Battery as a direct importation from Jerusalem, has his exclusive preserves at the lower end of Washington Street. The one thing you shall vainly ask for in the chief city of America is a distinctively American community. There is none; certainly not among the tenements. Where have they gone to, the old inhabitants? I put the question to one who might fairly be presumed to be of the number, since I found him sighing for the "good old days" when the legend "no Irish need apply" was familiar in the advertising columns of the newspapers. He looked at me with a puzzled air. "I don't know," he said. "... Some went to California in '49, some to the war and never came back. The rest ... have gone to heaven, or somewhere....

▲ A photograph, c.1912, of an Italian watch shop on Mott Street, which was located on the Lower East Side of New York City.

A GIFT FROM FRANCE

In a gesture of friendship and admiration, the people of France presented a gift to the United States that would become a symbol of freedom and of welcome to all those seeking a new home. Designed by French sculptor Frédéric-Auguste Bartholdi, the Statue of Liberty was unveiled in New York harbor on October 28, 1886. Its inscription reads:

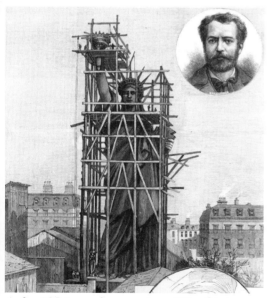

▲ An 1884 wood engraving of the Statue of Liberty being constructed. Bartholdi, the sculptor, is shown in the upper right.

Give me your tired, your poor,
Your huddled masses yearning
to breath free,
The wretched refuse of your
teeming shore.
Send these, the homeless,
tempest-tossed to me.
I lift my lamp beside the golden
door.

One of the speakers at the dedication was President Grover Cleveland, who said, "We will not forget that Liberty has made here her home, nor shall her chosen altar be neglected."

BLACKS CONTINUE TO STRUGGLE

While the new citizens of America saw a future full of promise, Southern blacks looked on helplessly. They saw very little improvement in their lives after slavery was abolished. The Civil Rights Act of 1875 prohibited racial discrimination in public places such as hotels, railroads, and theaters, but in 1883, the Supreme Court ruled it was invalid because it addressed social instead of civil rights. State legislatures all over the South began enacting laws that enforced racial segregation. The Supreme Court decision of *Plessy* v. *Ferguson* was a ruling that condoned the "separate but equal" doctrine. This decision would not be overturned until 1954.

66 … it couldn't have been intended to abolish distinctions based upon color… 99

PLESSY V. FERGUSON DECISION: 1896

… That [the Separate Car Act, Louisiana law which required blacks to sit in "colored" cars on trains] does not conflict with the Thirteenth Amendment, which abolished slavery … is too clear for argument.… A statute which implies merely a legal distinction between the white and colored races … has no tendency to destroy the legal equality of the two races.… The object of the [Fourteenth] amendment was … to enforce the absolute equality of the two races before the law, but … it couldn't have been intended to abolish distinctions based upon color, or to enforce social, as distinguished from political equality, or a commingling of the two races upon terms unsatisfactory to either.…

PUBLIC EDUCATION

Because immigrant parents wanted their children to go to school as a means to a better life, public school education doubled between 1870 and 1900. This increase contributed greatly to the sharp drop in illiteracy in the United States. New classes in American history and the sciences were added to the basic curriculum of reading, writing, and arithmetic.

Vocational training and higher education expanded, as well. The Morrill Act of 1862 donated land to the states to establish colleges of agriculture and mechanical arts. In 1890, a second Morrill Act initiated regular appropriations to support the land-grant colleges. Although the second Morrill Act forbade the use of race to deny admission to anyone, by allowing separate-but-equal institutions to be built, it did, in fact, do just that. With seventeen predominantly

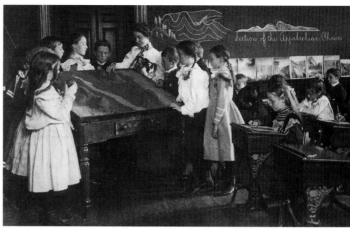

▲ This photograph taken at the turn of the century, shows a class in a Washington, D.C., public school.

black colleges and thirty American Indian colleges available, there was social pressure, sometimes even intimidation, for nonwhites to attend only nonwhite institutions.

SECOND MORRILL ACT: 1890

... That there shall be ... annually appropriated, out of any money in The Treasury ... from the sales of public lands; to be ... provided to each State and Territory for the more complete endowment and maintenance of colleges for the benefit of agriculture and the mechanic arts now established, or which may be hereafter established ... the sum of fifteen thousand dollars ... and an annual increase ... thereafter for ten years ... of one thousand dollars....

No money shall be paid out under this act ... for the maintenance of a college where a distinction of race or color is made in the admission of students, but the establishment and maintenance of such colleges separately for white and colored students shall be held to be a compliance with the provision of this act if the funds received in such State or Territory be equitably divided....

LEISURE TIME

With industrialization, Americans now had more leisure time. They went to sporting events, minstrel shows, concerts, and amusement parks. In 1893, many attended the World's Columbian Exposition in Chicago, where they marveled at the Exposition's cultural displays and artistic exhibits. People saw inventions such as the zipper and the Ferris Wheel, as well as innovations in architecture, machinery, and child care. Henry Adams, a visitor to the Exposition, wrote about his experiences there in a 1918 piece for the Massachusetts Historical Society.

THE EDUCATION OF HENRY ADAMS: 1918

... Education ran riot at Chicago, at least for ... minds which had never faced ... so many matters of which they were ignorant. [I saw] ... men who knew nothing whatever—who had never run a steam-engine, the simplest of forces—who had never put their hands on a lever—had never touched an electric battery—never talked through a telephone, and had not the shadow of a notion what amount of force was meant by a watt or an ampère or an erg, or any other term of measurement introduced within a hundred years....

▲ The Manufacturer's Building was just one of the exhibits at the Columbian Exposition of 1893, which was held in Chicago, Illinois.

Americans were also reading more. Realism was the central literary theme in the works of most American writers. In his most famous works— *The Adventures of Tom Sawyer* (1876) and *The Adventures of Huckleberry Finn* (1884)—Mark Twain wrote about life along the Mississippi River before the Civil War. William Dean Howells's *The Rise of Silas Lapham* (1885) described the newly rich American middle class. In *Maggie, A Girl of the*

Streets (1893), Stephen Crane tells the story of an innocent girl's struggle in the slums of New York City. Theodore Dreiser's *Sister Carrie* (1900) is the story of an independent small-town girl, who leaves her home for a factory job in the city and eventually becomes a successful, though unhappy, actress.

URBAN PROBLEMS

Although there was unimaginable wealth in urban America, there were also enormous problems. Immigrants moved into the poorer sections of the major cities, where the neighborhoods were overcrowded. This overcrowding contributed greatly to crime and the spread of disease. Some American-born citizens were also troubled by the influx of foreigners who didn't speak English. They saw these immigrants as threats to their jobs because the recent newcomers were willing to settle for lower wages.

In 1892, Giuseppe Giacosa, an Italian writer, visited the city of Chicago. He wrote about his impressions of the smoke-filled city—a condition that was caused by the burning of coal for residential heating and industrial power.

GIACOSA'S IMPRESSIONS OF CHICAGO: 1892

... I did not see in Chicago anything but darkness: smoke, clouds, dirt, and an extraordinary number of sad and grieved persons....

The rich metropolis gave me a sense of oppression so great that I still doubt whether, beyond [the] factories, there exist celestial spaces....

I saw them [Chicagoans] thus ... ill-tempered, [with a] pouting expression which I read on almost every face. They were running about desperately....

The dominant characteristic of the exterior life of Chicago is violence. Everything leads you to extreme expressions: dimensions, movements, noises, rumors, window displays, spectacles, ostentation, misery, activity, and alcoholic degradation....

66 The rich metropolis gave me a sense of oppression so great that I still doubt whether, beyond [the] factories, there exist celestial spaces.... 99

CHAPTER 5

The Gilded Age of Politics

1873–1900

In the latter half of the nineteenth century, Americans became dissatisfied with the greed of manufacturers, railroad managers, bankers, and wealthy men in general. Corruption was so widespread that, in 1874, when Mark Twain and Charles Dudley Warner satirized the United States as a land of shallow money grubbers in their novel *The Gilded Age*, the name stuck. Historians have used it to characterize this period in American history. The main political issues were monetary policy and civil service reform.

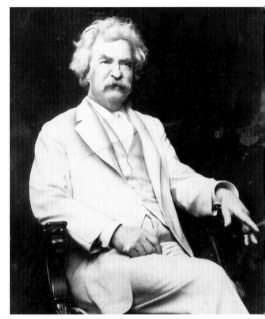

▲ A photograph, c.1907, of Mark Twain, who along with Charles Dudley Warner coined the phrase "The Gilded Age."

GOLD OR SILVER STANDARD?

The U.S. monetary system was in chaos after the Civil War. Congress knew if the country's paper currency were to have any real value when trading with other nations, it had to be backed up by a precious metal. What this meant was that anyone holding paper money could exchange it for the equivalent amount of that metal. By the 1870s, the currency controversy boiled down to which metal should be used: gold or silver.

Gold supporters believed its beauty and rarity made it almost magical. Silver supporters knew that it was this very rarity that would hinder prosperity by limiting the amount of money that could be in circulation. When gold was discovered in California in 1848, its market value suddenly decreased in relation to silver. People immediately started hoarding silver.

In 1873, Congress firmly tied the nation's monetary system to the gold standard. With the passage of the Specie Resumption Act in 1875, all currency in circulation, including paper money, was backed by gold. A major economic reversal in the fall of 1873, however, caused many Americans to barrage Congress with requests for assistance. They felt that since silver was more available than gold, their financial problems could be solved if silver were reinstated as legal tender.

In 1878, Richard P. Bland, a congressman from Missouri, was able to gain passage of a bill that provided for the liberal coinage of silver, but the more conservative Senate toned down the House proposal and with the support of Senator William B. Allison of Iowa agreed on the terms of what became the Bland-Allison Act.

The mining and debtor interests argued that the Bland-Allison Act did not go far enough, and they urged the free and unlimited coinage of silver. The gold supporters urged the repeal of the act and argued that economic stability could only be restored by strict adherence to the gold standard. President Rutherford B. Hayes, who

BLAND-ALLISON ACT: 1878

… That there shall be coined, at the several mints of the United States, silver dollars of the weight of four hundred and twelve and a half grains of Troy of standard silver.… The Secretary of the Treasury is authorized and directed to purchase, from time to time, silver bullions at the market price thereof, not less than two million dollars per month, nor more than four million dollars worth per month, and cause the same to be coined monthly, as fast as so purchased into such dollars.…

was influenced by industrial and banking interests, vetoed the measure, but Congress promptly overrode the veto. The Hayes administration blunted the impact of it, however, by purchasing only the minimum amount of silver each month.

Congress reintroduced legislation in 1890 with the Sherman Silver Purchase Act, which was part of a broader compromise. The measure allowed the Treasury to buy silver each month at the market rate and to issue notes redeemable in either gold or silver. This increased the supply of silver and drove down the price.

As the price of silver continued to decline, holders of government notes redeemed them for gold rather than silver, which depleted the gold reserves of the United States.

At the Democratic Convention in 1896, the nation's monetary policy was the most important issue. William Jennings Bryan, a former congressman from Nebraska, endorsed the free coinage of silver, which would increase the amount of money in circulation and help debt-burdened farmers. Bryan's "Cross of Gold" speech not only helped defeat a platform resolution in favor of the gold standard but also earned him the Democratic nomination for the presidency. Bryan lost to the Republican candidate, William McKinley. In 1900, McKinley signed the Gold Standard Act, which required that all paper money be backed by gold.

(In 1971, the United States abandoned the gold standard, although it retained its holdings of the metal because it is still an internationally recognized commodity. Since 1976, the United States no longer sets the gold value of a dollar. The price of gold rises and falls in relation to the demand for the metal.)

BRYAN'S "CROSS OF GOLD" SPEECH: 1896

▲ William Jennings Bryan photographed during his run for the presidency in 1896.

… You come to us and tell us that the great cities are in favor of the gold standard; we reply that the great cities rest upon our broad and fertile prairies. Burn down your cities and leave our farms, and your cities will spring up again as if by magic; but destroy our farms and the grass will grow in the streets of every city.…

No, my friends, that will never be the verdict.… If they … come out in the open field and defend the gold standard as a good thing, we will fight them to the uttermost.… You shall not press down upon the brow of labor this crown of thorns, you shall not crucify mankind upon a cross of gold.

CIVIL SERVICE REFORM

Angered by the scandals of the Grant administration and political corruption in general, U.S. citizens demanded a change in the way government jobs were given out. The "Stalwarts" believed in the spoils system, where the party in power replaced all office holders in the government with members of its own party. The "Half-Breeds" wanted to put an end to this patronage. In 1880, Republicans nominated James A. Garfield, a Half-Breed, for president and Chester A. Arthur, a Stalwart, for vice president.

Garfield won the election, but four months later, he was assassinated by a Stalwart, and Vice President Arthur became president. In reaction to the assassination, Congress passed the Pendleton Civil Service Act, which created an independent Civil Service Commission and determined which jobs in the federal government would be filled on a merit basis instead of by political appointment. The number of positions covered by the law was small at first, but later legislation expanded the number and improved the quality of federal employees.

THE PENDLETON CIVIL SERVICE ACT: 1883

... It shall be the duty of said commissioners ... [to arrange for] open, competitive examinations for testing the fitness of applicants for the public service....

That all the offices, places and employments so arranged ... shall be filled by selections according to grade from among those graded highest as the results of such competitive examinations....

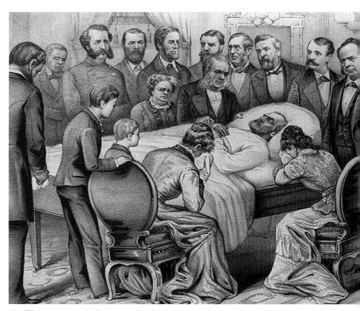

▲ This 1881 lithograph depicts the death of President James A. Garfield. His wound may not have been fatal were it not for the incompetence of his doctors.

THE POPULIST PARTY

Most farmers believed that railroads, banks, and others with whom they did business overcharged them, so several farmers met in Ocala, Florida, in 1890 to develop a political platform. It was adopted when the Populist party was formally organized in 1892.

Its platform called for an eight-hour workday and immigration restrictions, condemned the use of private detectives against striking workers, and supported such political reforms as the secret ballot. It also called for the railroads to be nationalized.

THE OCALA DEMANDS: 1890

We demand the abolition of national banks.

We demand that the government shall ... loan money direct to the people at a low rate of interest....

We demand that Congress shall pass such laws as will effectually prevent the dealing in futures of all agricultural and mechanical productions....

We condemn the silver bill recently passed by Congress, and demand in lieu thereof the free and unlimited coinage of silver.

We demand the passage of laws prohibiting alien ownership of land....

We demand that the Congress ... submit an amendment to the Constitution ... for the election of ... Senators by direct vote of the people of each state.

Although the Populist party elected five senators and ten representatives, Democrat Grover Cleveland took the White House for a second term in 1892.

Shortly thereafter, the nation was hit by an economic crisis, which Cleveland was unable to bring under control. The crisis was triggered by the bankruptcy of several railroads and the failure of a British bank that caused many British investors to exchange their American stocks for gold.

Prosperity Returns under William McKinley

By the time William McKinley became president in 1896, the crisis had almost run its course—and with it the extreme agitation over silver. In the friendly atmosphere of the McKinley administration, industries grew at an unprecedented pace and farm prices began to increase. In an 1888 article from a monthly journal called *The Manufacturer and Builder*, the iron industry is shown growing at a remarkable pace at this time.

Growth of the Iron and Steel Industries: 1888

The inspection of the figures exhibiting the production of iron and steel in the United States during the past year ... tells the story of such wonderful progress as has never been paralleled in any other great industry in this country....

In spite of this enormous increase in production it is specially significant that the general range of prices was kept within very reasonable bounds, a fact which was due to the greatly increased capacity of our domestic iron and steel works....

▲ William McKinley ran on a platform based on prosperity. This 1900 campaign poster shows him standing on a gold coin of "sound money."

Despite McKinley's support of big business, he gave priority to labor unions and aimed his policies at the well-being of ordinary citizens. He was also one of the most fervent defenders of civil rights for black Americans.

By the end of the century, the United States had surpassed all other countries as the world's leading industrial nation. Now, the United States began to turn its attention to a new issue: overseas expansion.

CHAPTER 6

Imperial America

1867–1900

Although the United States had been concerned primarily with domestic issues in the years before, during, and following the Civil War, it did manage to acquire in, 1857, several small islands in the Pacific that were to be used as coaling stations for American ships.

By 1870 in Europe, the countries of Great Britain, France, Belgium, Germany, and Italy had already seized territory and established colonies in Africa and Asia. Just about that time, the United States was also ready to do the same thing in the Caribbean and the Pacific. The purchase of Alaska from Russia in 1867 was seen as an important step in opening Asian markets to American goods. In 1878, a naval station was established at Pago Pago in Samoa.

In 1887, the United States built a naval base at Pearl Harbor in the Hawaiian chain of islands. Shortly thereafter, Americans who owned sugar plantations on the islands demanded that the Hawaiian rulers establish a constitutional monarchy under American control. Queen Liliuokalani tried to reassert Hawaiian sovereignty, but the planters staged a successful coup and proclaimed the Republic of

HAWAII'S EX-QUEEN FILES A PROTEST

Mrs. Dominis Demands That the Treaty Be Declared Void for Many Reasons.

THE CLEVELAND EPISODE

Refers to That as the Main Reason to Be Urged Against the Ratification of the Treaty.

EX-QUEEN LILIOUKALANI

◀ **An 1897 newspaper clipping of Queen Liliuokalani protesting the anticipated U.S. annexation of Hawaii.**

... The Government of the Republic of Hawaii having ... signified its consent ... to cede absolutely and without reserve to the United States of America all rights of sovereignty ... over the Hawaiian Islands and their dependencies ... and to cede ... the absolute ... ownership of all public, government, or Crown lands, public buildings or edifices, ports, harbors, military equipment, and all other public property of every description ... therefore that said cession is accepted, ratified, and confirmed, and ... the said Hawaiian Islands ... are hereby annexed as a part of the territory of the United States....

"... the said Hawaiian Islands ... are hereby annexed as part of the territory of the United States...."

Hawaii on July 4, 1894. The United States quickly recognized the new republic, but the matter did not end there. William McKinley called for annexation of the islands. There were protests from native Hawaiian citizens and others who were in sympathy with Queen Liliuokalani. On October 8, 1897, the largest organized gathering ever of Hawaiian royalists met in Palace Square to protest the anticipated annexation of Hawaii by the United States. They appealed to the principles of human rights, to the U.S. Constitution, and to international law as a way to convince the American government to abandon its plans to annex the islands and to return the queen to her throne. Despite these protestations, Hawaii officially became a U.S. territory in 1900.

▲ A photograph in 1898 shows the lowering of the Hawaiian flag on top of Iolani Palace in Honolulu. The American flag was then raised in its place.

JUSTIFICATIONS FOR EXPANSION

One of the main reasons for the nation's participation in the Age of Imperialism was economics. Foreign markets were needed to ensure continued economic growth of the country—and for national prestige.

Business leaders had a strong belief that they could make huge profits by selling American goods abroad, especially in the nations of Central and South America and of Asia. The success of the American sugarcane planters in Hawaii also proved that direct investment in the development of the natural resources of those countries could be very profitable.

Those Americans who recognized the value of overseas trade also advocated a strong navy. In 1890, Captain Alfred Thayer Mahan wrote in his book *The Influence of Sea Power upon History, 1660–1783,* that a nation's greatness depended on its navy and that only those countries with the greatest fleets would play a decisive role in shaping history.

Captain Mahan's vision for the United States included overseas colonies and the control of a canal that would link the Atlantic and Pacific Oceans, either across Panama or Nicaragua in Central America. The ideas that Mahan espoused influenced men such as Theodore Roosevelt, who served as assistant secretary of the navy under President McKinley, and Senator Henry Cabot Lodge, who was a supporter of American expansion.

THE INFLUENCE OF SEA POWER UPON HISTORY: 1890

… From time to time the superstructure of tactics has to be altered or wholly torn down; but the old foundations of strategy so far remain, as though laid upon a rock.…

Whether they will or no, Americans must now begin to look outward. The growing production of the country demands it.…

The [nation] which controls the seas controls its own fate.…

Those [nations] that lack naval mastery are doomed to defeat or the second rank [of nations].…

Whoever rules the waves rules the world.…

THE SPANISH-AMERICAN WAR

Cuban discontent with Spanish rule flared into open revolt in 1895, when the island experienced an economic depression. Cuban revolutionaries hoped the United States would intervene, but President Cleveland announced a policy of neutrality.

The few Americans who had large financial interests in Cuba did not want the United States to intervene because they believed that Spain would eventually restore stability to the island. But some prominent newspapers printed exaggerated accounts of Spanish atrocities to increase their papers' circulation and, in doing so, affected public opinion in favor of U.S. intervention.

Support for war with Spain was fueled when, on February 9, 1898, the *New York Journal* printed a private letter that was written by the Spanish minister to the United States, Enrique Dupuy De Lome, to a friend in Cuba. This communication contained slurs against President McKinley, and it strained the relationship between the two countries even more.

THE DE LOME LETTER: 1898

Eximo Señor Don José Cañalejas:
My Distinguished and Dear Friend:

You need not apologize for not having written to me; I also ought to have written to you, but have not done so on account of being weighed down with work....

The situation here continues unchanged. Everything depends on the political and military success in Cuba....

Besides the natural and inevitable coarseness with which he [President McKinley] repeats all that the press and public opinion of Spain has said of Weyler [Spanish general in Cuba], it shows once more what McKinley is: weak and catering to the rabble, and ... a low politician, who desires to leave a door open to me and to stand well with the jingoes of his party....

"... it shows once more what McKinley is: weak and catering to the rabble...."

Congress demanded that the Spanish government recall the diplomat. Just a few days after the letter appeared, the United States battleship *Maine* blew up in Havana harbor, killing two hundred and sixty men. Although the cause of the explosion was never determined, Spain was blamed. Americans demanded retribution, and on April 25, 1898, President McKinley declared war on Spain.

DECLARATION OF WAR BETWEEN THE UNITED STATES OF AMERICA AND SPAIN: 1898

… Be it enacted … First. That War be, and the same is hereby, declared to exist, and that war has existed since … [April 21] including said day, between the United States of America and the Kingdom of Spain.

… Second. That the President of the United States be, and he hereby is, directed and empowered to use the entire land and naval forces of the United States, and to call into the actual service of the United States the militia of the several States, to such extent as may be necessary to carry this Act into effect.…

▲ The wreck of the *Maine* in Havana after it was decorated in 1902.

The first victory of the war came far from Cuba. The United States captured the entire Spanish fleet in the Battle of Manila Bay, on May 1, 1898, and with the help of Filipino insurrectionists, took control of Manila.

In June, seventeen thousand U.S. troops landed in Cuba. Among them was a cavalry regiment known as the "Rough Riders." It was under the command of Theodore Roosevelt. Within a few weeks, American forces

◀ An undated print depicts Colonel Theodore Roosevelt leading his calvary regiment called the Rough Riders.

had captured every strategic location on the island. By the end of July, Spain was asking for peace. The Spanish-American War came to a close with the Treaty of Paris on December 10, 1898. Spain gave up its claims to Cuba and ceded several islands, including Puerto Rico, Guam, Wake Island, and the Philippine Islands to the United States.

TREATY OF PARIS: 1898

... Spain relinquishes all claim of sovereignty over and title to Cuba.... The island ... upon its evacuation by Spain ... [will be occupied] by the United States....

Spain cedes to the United States the island of Porto [Puerto] Rico and the other islands now under Spanish sovereignty in the West Indies, and the island of Guam in the Marianas....

Spain cedes to the United States ... the Philippine Islands....

The United States will ... send back to Spain, at its own cost, the Spanish soldiers taken as prisoners of war....

Spain will ... release all prisoners of war, and all persons detained ... in connection with the insurrections in Cuba and the Philippines and the war with the United States....

❝... Spain relinquishes all claim of sovereignty over and title to Cuba....❞

PHILIPPINE-AMERICAN WAR

After the Spanish-American War, the Filipinos expected the United States to grant them independence, but when that didn't happen, a revolt against American rule began. Also known as the Philippine Insurrection, the Philippine-American War was based mostly on guerrilla tactics. It lasted until 1901, when the Philippine president Emilio Aguinaldo surrendered.

PROCLAMATION OF FORMAL SURRENDER TO THE UNITED STATES: 1901

... I believe that ... the complete termination of hostilities and a lasting peace are not only desirable but absolutely essential to the welfare of the Philippines....

By acknowledging and accepting the sovereignty of the United States throughout the entire Archipelago ... I believe that I am serving thee, my beloved country. May happiness be thine!

▲ A photograph, c.1899, shows the burning of a Philippine village, which was part of the practice of guerrilla warfare.

OPEN DOOR POLICY

At the end of the nineteenth century, China was in political and economic disarray. It was not recognized as a sovereign nation by the major powers—Great Britain, France, Germany, Russia, and Japan—who were busy vying with one another for trading privileges and plotting how China could be partitioned. Since the United States did not want to be left out of this lucrative market, in the fall of 1898, President McKinley indicated his desire for an "open door" policy that would allow all trading nations access to the Chinese market.

The Chinese felt they were being suffocated by the stronger imperialist nations. This resentment intensified among members of a secret group called *I Ho Chuan*, or "the society of righteous fists." The English translation of the group's name was the "boxers," and their revolt was called the Boxer Rebellion. The Boxers raided trading outposts and Christian missions, killing all Westerners. An international expeditionary force, under the command of the United States, was sent to Peking to put down the rebellion. As punishment, China was forced to disarm and to pay almost $400 million in reparations.

THE OPEN DOOR NOTES: 1899–1900

Earnestly desirous to remove any cause of irritation and to insure ... the commerce to all nations in China ... [the United States urges all nations claiming a sphere of influence in China to declare] that [all nations] shall enjoy perfect equality of treatment for their commerce and navigation within such spheres....

[The United States seeks] the adoption of measures insuring the benefits of equality ... of all foreign trade throughout China....

▲ A 1900 lithograph depicting the Allied armies of the United States, England, Germany, Russia, and Japan entering the Peking Palace during the Boxer Rebellion.

TIME LINE

1867	■ The United States acquires Alaska from Russia.
1868	■ President Andrew Johnson is impeached but is acquitted at his trial.
1868	■ Ulysses S. Grant is elected the eighteenth U.S. president.
1869	■ The Central Pacific and the Union Pacific Railroads are joined, creating the first transcontinental railroad.
1870	■ The Fifteenth Amendment to the Constitution gives black men the right to vote.
1876	■ Rutherford B. Hayes is elected the nineteenth U.S. president.
1880	■ James A. Garfield is elected the twentieth U.S. president, but dies in office; Vice President Chester A. Arthur becomes the twenty-first U.S. president in 1881.
1884	■ Grover Cleveland is elected the twenty-second U.S. president.
1886	■ France gives the Statue of Liberty to the United States.
1888	■ Benjamin Harrison is elected the twenty-third U.S. president.
1889	■ Settlers race to claim free land in the Oklahoma Land Run.
1890	■ The Sherman Antitrust Act is passed, prohibiting commercial monopolies.
1890	■ The Battle at Wounded Knee ends the Indian Wars.
1896	■ The Supreme Court decision in *Plessy* v. *Ferguson* holds that racial segregation is constitutional.
1896	■ William McKinley is elected the twenty-fifth U.S. president.
1898	■ The United States annexes Hawaii.
1898	■ The USS *Maine* is blown up in Havana harbor; the United States declares war on Spain.
1898	■ The Spanish-American War ends; the United States gains control of Puerto Rico, Guam, and the Philippines.
1899	■ Filipinos fight for independence in the Philippine-American War.
1900	■ Chinese Boxers attempt to rid their country of imperialist nations.

Glossary

amnesty: a pardon.

annexation: incorporation of one country into another.

antitrust: to oppose big business monopolies.

black codes: laws in the South after the Civil War meant to limit the rights of blacks.

civil service: nonmilitary employment in government.

cooperatives: jointly owned facilities or services.

emancipation: the act of freeing people from slavery.

executive branch: part of government headed by the president.

expeditionary: military.

foreclosures: takeovers of people's properties because of failure to make payments.

Ghost Dance: ritual among Plains Indians during the late 1800s.

gold standard: backing a nation's paper money with gold.

Grange: farmer's support organization.

homestead: land claimed by settlers.

impeach: to accuse a government official of improper conduct.

imperialism: acquisition of another nation through conquest.

insurrection: a revolt.

interstate: between two or more states.

intimidation: threats.

jingoes: people who favor a threatening foreign policy.

Ku Klux Klan: white supremacist organization formed after the Civil War.

land run: race to claim free land in Oklahoma.

monopolize: for one company to completely control a service.

naturalized: not born in the country of residence.

open door policy: policy that made trade with China available to all nations.

patronage: the act of granting appointments to office.

philanthropist: person who gives a lot of his or her own money to people or organizations.

platform: principles declared by a speaker or political party.

populist: supporting the needs of the common people.

reaper: a machine for harvesting grain.

Reconstruction: period of rebuilding, after the Civil War.

severalty: condition of being given the right to own land.

strikes: work stoppages in protest of perceived unfair business practices.

tenure: length of time someone has been at his or her job.

urban: pertaining to cities.

FURTHER INFORMATION

BOOKS

Hanson, Joyce. *Bury Me Not in a Land of Slaves: African-Americans in the Time of Reconstruction*. Franklin Watts/Grolier, 2000.

Hook, Jason. *To Live and Die in the West: The American Indian Wars 1860-90*. Osprey Publishing Company, 2000.

Noyes, Martha H. *Then There Were None*. Bess Press, 2003.

WEB SITES

www.memory.loc.gov/ammem/ndlpedu/features/timeline/civilwar/civilwar.html This Web site highlights the Civil War and Reconstruction and is part of the Library of Congress's American Memory Historical Collection for the National Digital Library. It presents reference information as well as hands-on activities for students.

www.smplanet.com/imperialism/toc.html This Web site presents historical information as well as maps and images on the era of U.S. imperialism.

USEFUL ADDRESSES

The Friends of Iolani Palace (official residence of Queen Liliuokalani)
P.O. Box 2259
Honolulu, HI 96804
Telephone: (808) 522-0832

National Museum of the American Indian
4th Street and Independence Avenue, SW
Washington, DC 20024
Telephone: (202) 633-1000

★ ★ ★ INDEX ★ ★ ★

MANCOS
PUBLIC LIBRARY

Severance Middle School
Media Center

38204000038124